The Adult Coloring Book

Richard Muraoka

About the Author

This is the first time I am designing coloring book. I am excited to publish this on the market. Enjoy, keep it simple

Dedication

I like to dedicate all the people

enjoy coloring. keep it simple

Notes

Notes

www.ingramcontent.com/pod-product-compliance
Lightning Source LLC
Chambersburg PA
CBHW041831280526
45792CB00006B/2046

9 781533 085788